MW01075399

COLLECTION

GROWING THROUGH THE MOTIONS

LIVING YOUR FAITH WITH INTENTION

FR. MIKE SCHMITZ

ASCENSION
West Chester, Pennsylvania

Unless otherwise noted, Scripture passages are from the Revised Standard Version–Second Catholic Edition © 2006 by the Division of Christian Education of the National Council of the Churches of Christ in the United States of America. Used by permission. All rights reserved.

Ascension
PO Box 1990
West Chester, PA 19380
1-800-376-0520
ascensionpress.com

Cover design: James Kegley

Printed in the United States of America

ISBN 978-1-954882-98-0 (trade book)
ISBN 978-1-954882-99-7 (e-book)

CONTENTS

WELCOME TO THE SUNDAY HOMILIES WITH FR. MIKE SCHMITZ COLLECTION

Each booklet in this series has been created to invite Catholics to grow closer to God through reflections from Fr. Mike.

These booklets are short and relatable, with features that will help you apply what you read to your own life.

Quotes and Bible verses throughout the booklets will help you zero in on the key points.

Questions after each section prompt you to reflect and help you to dive deeper into the topic being presented. We recommend that you pray or journal with these questions as you make connections to your everyday life. (They also make great prompts for small group discussion, while keeping in mind that not everyone in your group may feel comfortable answering those of a more personal nature.)

Meditations are provided after each reflection to help you take the topic directly into prayer. We recommend setting aside some time after each chapter to read the meditation and pray or journal with it.

Each reflection ends with a challenge to put what you have learned into action. These challenges invite you to enter into prayer, serve others, make a resolution for the week, and more.

It is our sincere hope **The Sunday Homilies with Fr. Mike Schmitz Collection** helps you along the way in your journey toward holiness. May God bless you!

*Note: This booklet is adapted from a series of homilies given by Fr. Mike Schmitz.

CHAPTER 1

PASSION OR DUTY?

When Queen Elizabeth II died at age ninety-six, almost everything people had to say about her was positive.

I remember one quote that said, "She never made the mistake of thinking that she was an interesting or remarkable person in herself, and thereby she became remarkable."[1] She never thought that she was a queen due to her own greatness. She wasn't deceived into thinking that she had earned her position but realized that being the queen was an accident of birth and circumstances.

She wasn't even supposed to be queen. Elizabeth's uncle abdicated the throne when she was a little girl, and her dad became King George VI. There is an account of her younger sister, Margaret, asking, "Does this mean you'll be the queen?" And in a really British way, Elizabeth said, "Yes, I suppose it does." That was it. Margaret said they never talked about it again until Elizabeth became queen at age twenty-five.

From age twenty-five to age ninety-six, this woman showed up every single day. She didn't do it because being the queen was her ambition, or because she had always dreamed of it, but simply because she was asked.

Almost every article I read about Queen Elizabeth said that she simply did her duty. Of course, you could say, "Well, she had pretty good working conditions, I mean, a couple of palaces." Yet, at the same time, you and I know what it is like to do something simply because you have to. Not because you want to, not because you dream of doing it, but because someone asked you to do it.

QUEEN ELIZABETH II
April 21, 1926–September 8, 2022

Queen Elizabeth II was not only the longest-reigning monarch in British history, on the throne for over seventy years, but she was also much-loved across the world and known for being grounded in her Christian faith.

When we are given a duty—something we have to do—what is our usual response? What's our attitude when we're obliged to do something?

When I was a kid, I had to help out with chores. My mom would sometimes watch when I was sweeping the floor and say, "What are you doing? You're just pushing the dirt around." Or, when I would have to vacuum a room, she would say, "You were done in three minutes. It takes a lot longer than that to vacuum." Whether it is household chores, busy work at our jobs, or any other task that we don't choose for ourselves, we're tempted to do the work halfheartedly. When we're obliged to do something, our attitude is often that we only sort of do it.

We will do what is asked of us, but only by going through the motions. How much of our life is spent just going through the motions?

How much of our life is spent just going through the motions?

When it comes to faith, our attitude toward so much of what we do is often, "I have to be here, I know I'm obliged." We know it's our duty, and so we end up going through the motions. This can become the thing that defines our relationship with God, and we end up stuck. Have you ever felt this way when it comes to your faith?

I wonder if this is what moved the disciples when they asked Jesus to increase their faith (see Luke 17:5). I wonder if they looked at their faith and realized, "I feel stuck, I don't want to be here," and asked for more faith. I imagine that even those disciples who lived with Jesus could have felt like they were going through the motions sometimes.

Even Paul, writing to Timothy, says, "I remind you to rekindle the gift of God that is within you" (2 Timothy 1:6). Just like the disciples, Timothy might have felt stuck in his faith. Paul wants more for Timothy, and the disciples want more for themselves. They all want to be unstuck. This idea that you can "rekindle" your gifts—that you can increase in faith—tells us that if you are stuck, you don't have to stay stuck.

Choose to start *growing* through the motions.

If you feel like you are going through the motions, if you feel stuck in your faith, realize that faith can grow. If it can grow, it's alive, which means that you can do something about it. God wants your faith to grow. But you also have agency, which means that you can do something to get unstuck. You can take steps to grow your faith. Rather than just showing up and going through the motions, we can choose to live differently and start *growing* through the motions.

So many people, whether they were raised in the Church or just recently came into the Faith, get to a point where they feel like they know everything, and they feel stuck. It doesn't have to be this way. We can choose to grow through the motions.

"WAX ON, WAX OFF"

Whenever I think of going through the motions, I think of *The Karate Kid*.

In the original movie, this kid named Daniel LaRusso moves from New Jersey to California, with his mom. He has trouble adjusting and making friends. On his first day of school, he gets bullied, picked on, and beaten up.

Then he meets a man named Mr. Miyagi who can teach him karate. I'll paraphrase their first conversation. Daniel shows up at Mr. Miyagi's house for his first lesson, and Mr. Miyagi says, "I'll teach you karate. Here's what you need to do: Paint the fence. Paint long strokes. Paint up and down." Once Daniel finishes, Mr. Miyagi says, "I need you to wax the car. Like this: wax on, wax off. After that, I need you to sand the deck."

After days of working on these tasks, Daniel gets frustrated. It all seems meaningless. He wanted to learn karate, but Mr. Miyagi is teaching him how to paint a fence, how to wax a car, and how to sand a deck. So, one last time, Mr. Miyagi asks him to paint the fence. As Daniel moves to do it, Mr. Miyagi punches at him. Daniel blocks him. He hadn't realized it, but painting the fence is a block for a punch. And waxing the car turns out to be a block for a kick.[2]

Whatever the skill, practice does something. But it doesn't work if you don't know the point. If someone says, "Paint the fence using long strokes," but doesn't tell me why, eventually I'll get sloppy and start painting sideways. Instead of waxing the car in the way I was shown, I'll start scrubbing side to side to get it done faster. If I don't know the point, the movements just become meaningless tasks.

We sometimes feel this way when we come to Mass. Everything we do at Mass has a point. It is all supposed to mean something, but most of the time, we do it simply because it is our duty. We have no idea what it means. Just imagine how different our worship at Mass could be if we realized the meaning.

If our actions are not meaningful, then mere duty is slavery. Going through the motions becomes a trap because merely doing your duty is a recipe for discouragement and burnout. The solution would seem to be just avoiding duty, and this is a temptation, but it is not the answer. In fact, the truly heroic among us are those who do the right thing even when they don't feel like it.

The truly heroic among us are those who do the right thing even when they don't feel like it.

On September 11, 2001, when the Twin Towers were burning and collapsing, most people were running out of the buildings. But some people ran into the buildings. Many of those people died. Afterward, during interviews, the people who ran back into the buildings and survived said that they did not view what they did as being heroic. They said they were doing what they were supposed to do—what anyone else would have done. And many were quoted as saying, "I simply did my duty." Now, whether they were doing their duty required by them for a job description of a first responder, or doing their duty as a human being with a conscience and moral obligation to help others in their time of need, or even both, we all view their actions and those of the people who died that day running back into the buildings as heroic. But isn't it interesting to hear those who risked their own lives to save others not view themselves as heroes but as people just doing their "duty"? Duty is not the enemy. According to the Gospel, it is the minimum. But doing anything for duty alone is also not the point, because a duty is meaningless without any purpose. And that's how it can be if we only show up to Mass because it's our "duty."

PUT YOUR HEART INTO IT

When we say we are just "going through the motions," the motions are not the problem. The problem is our perspective.

Think about this. In the Gospel of Luke, the disciples say to Jesus, "Increase our faith" (Luke 17:5). Maybe you ask the same thing at Mass. What is faith? Sometimes, we mistakenly believe that faith is a quantifiable item. We imagine ourselves having faith tanks like gas tanks. We want to say, "Lord, my faith tank is getting low, so fill me up, increase my faith."

But faith is not a *thing*. Faith is *trust*. Faith is trust in another, which means that you can't hold onto it—it is a relationship. So if I ask God to increase my faith, I am asking God to strengthen my relationship with him. Faith is also not a feeling. The Apostles were not asking Jesus to increase their feeling. It's not as if one day they said, "Jesus, it's nice to be with you and everything, but I'm not feeling it anymore, so, could you increase that feeling in me?"

Faith is not a *thing*. Faith is not a feeling. Faith is *trust*.

And St. Paul, writing to Timothy, does not tell him to rekindle a feeling (2 Timothy 1:6). This is so important. The question is not, "What does faith feel like?" The question is, "What does faith do?" St. Paul says to Timothy, "God did not give us a spirit of timidity but a spirit of power and love and self-control" (2 Timothy 1:7). Power, love, and self-control are not feelings, they're ways of living.

> "God did not give us a spirit of timidity but a spirit of power and love and self-control" (2 Timothy 1:7).

Some of the most spirit-led people I know are exorcists. When we think about exorcists, we usually imagine that they are super holy, incredibly gifted, and incredibly talented. That might be the case. But for the most part, those who are involved in the ministry of exorcism are not special aside from the fact that they are spirit-led people who walk in power, love, and self-control. And this is because every single one of them has to walk in faith every day. Every time they go into an exorcism, they have to trust that God will act. So every time they pray, they are expecting God to act, and they are pushing the limits of their faith at every exorcism.

Exorcists simply pray out of the Rite of Exorcism. They are saying prayers that you and I could pray ourselves. The difference is that when you and I pray, a lot of times we are just going through the motions. We're praying because it's our duty, but our hearts are not in it.

When exorcists are praying, they are putting their hearts into it. Every time they pray, they are walking in faith, stretching their trust in God to the very edge, because their lives depend on it. Imagine how our lives would change if we showed up and prayed like that, and if we pushed ourselves to the very limits of our faith.

DELIBERATE PRACTICE

Years ago, a scientist named Anders Ericsson studied people who are experts in their fields. He discerned that most experts have a couple things in common. One thing is that all of them put in at least ten thousand hours of practice in order to become excellent.

Journalist Malcolm Gladwell popularized Anders Ericsson's findings in his book *Outliers*. In the book, he goes through examples of all these successful people, like the Beatles. Even though the Beatles seemed like an overnight sensation, as if one day they just exploded on the scene, they had put in well over ten thousand hours performing in bars throughout Europe before anyone had ever heard of them. So, when they showed up on the scene, they knew exactly what they were doing.[3]

The same is true for Bill Gates. Unlike almost anyone else in the world at the time, Bill Gates had access to computer programming when he was thirteen years old. From age thirteen to age twenty-three, he put in over ten thousand hours of computer programming, so that by the time he started Microsoft, he was arguably the world's expert in programming. A version of this story is true for every expert in every field.

Ericsson and Gladwell made one thing clear: it doesn't just take ten thousand hours of practice to become an expert, it takes ten thousand hours of *deliberate* practice. I started playing guitar when I was a freshman in college, and for the first four years, I got really good. Now, thirty years later, I play the guitar occasionally, but I am a worse guitar player than I was as a senior in college. I was at my peak after four years. Why? Because I spent that time learning so many new things. Every time I picked up my guitar, I was pushing the limits of my ability to play. When I pick up my guitar now, I'm OK, but I just play the songs I already know. I have not grown at all in playing the guitar since my senior year.

The same is true for so many of us. We might peak at one point, but then we realize that we're stuck. This is not because we aren't going through the motions, but because we're not *growing* through the motions. It's not about passion or duty. We grow when we show up and go through the motions and put our whole heart into it.

One of the things that made Queen Elizabeth II great was that she lived her life in a unique way. She lived as if she had actually chosen it. She did her duty and carried out her obligations as if it mattered. Even though she went through the motions, her heart was in it. And that makes all the difference.

As Catholics worshipping at Mass, everything we do is to create saints. That's a worthy goal. It's not mere passion or duty, but carrying out our duties with our whole hearts, confident that we are doing meaningful tasks for a worthy purpose. If we can have this perspective, going through the motions changes into something incredible. We don't have to be stuck. We can grow through the motions.

REFLECT

Reflect on a specific time in your life when you were asked to do something out of a sense of duty. How did you approach it? Did you put your whole heart into it, or did you find yourself just going through the motions?

Consider Queen Elizabeth II's reign. What details of her life did critics praise after her death? What can you conclude about the relationship between humility and putting your heart into a task?

Deliberate practice is key to becoming an expert in any field. How can you apply this concept to your spiritual life? What deliberate practices can help you grow in your faith?

With the right perspective, everyday practices can lead you to sainthood. How can you strive to live with this goal in mind?

PRAY

Your life is most likely filled with duties and responsibilities on all fronts, and often the weight of things you "have to do" can feel like it is going to crush you. This chapter offers you God's way of handling your burden, not by shirking your duty, but by offering your heart to God through it.

Paul's letter to the Colossians says, "Whatever your task, work heartily, as serving the Lord and not men" (Colossians 3:23). As you begin your time of prayer, take a moment to think of your heaviest duty, your most stressful responsibility. Think of the irritation, feelings of inadequacy, and even the fear that it brings. Think of the people you have a duty to. Keep all of that heaviness in front of you, with God at your side.

Now comes the difficult and beautiful part. Instead of asking God to make your burden lighter or take away your responsibility, ask the Holy Spirit to show you how you can put your heart into the duty and responsibility you have. Ask God how you can love him more by fulfilling your duty. Be prepared to put into action whatever the Lord puts on your heart, a heart filled with love for him. Do it for the Lord!

ACT ///

Choose two or three elements of the Mass to reflect on (for example, the readings, the Creed, the responsorial psalm, the offertory, etc.). Arrive at Mass early this week and prayerfully reflect on the significance of these elements before Mass begins.

CHAPTER 2

START WITH WHY

I recently had a conversation with a college freshman. I asked her what she was majoring in, and she said that she didn't know.

I asked, "What would you like to do after college?"
She said, "I don't know."
"What are you interested in?"
"I don't know."

Then I asked, "Well, what brought you here?" And she said, "It's just what you do. College was the next step, and so here I am."

I am not picking on her. This is super common. A lot of times, the only reason we show up anywhere is because we feel that we are supposed to. We spend so much of our lives doing "the next thing."

When you went to school, you probably started with preschool. Then you moved to kindergarten. After kindergarten, you went on to first grade, second grade, and all the way up to twelfth grade. Then, you went on to college or trade school. It was the next thing for you, because at that point, you knew how to be a student. That's really good.

The problem is that we can live our entire lives like this. We can spend a lifetime just showing up and doing what we know how to do. Ultimately, we may not know why we are in a certain job or relationship beyond the reason that at the time, it just made sense. It was the next thing to do.

We can spend a lifetime just showing up and doing what we know how to do.

When it comes to church and faith, we can easily slip into thinking this way. At Mass, it is really easy to believe that we are simply going through the motions. Every Sunday, we walk in, we genuflect, and we make the Sign of the Cross. When we hear, "The Lord be with you," we know what to say. We know what to do and how to do it.

FINDING YOUR "WHY"

Author and speaker Simon Sinek explains that corporations and businesses operate this way, too. They know what they're doing and how to do it. But, he says, exceptional organizations know *why*. In his book, *Start with Why*, he explains that if you don't want to be like everyone else who just goes through the motions, you have to ask the question, "Why am I doing this?"[4]

That's why this book is called *Growing Through the Motions*. This is what we have to do. Otherwise, our daily routines can feel empty, meaningless, and mundane.

In a normal week, you get up, you go to work, you come home, and you go to bed, and then for the next four days, you repeat it all over again. The day after that, it's the weekend, and you stay in bed. But on Monday, you get up and you go to work. It's a whole cycle of "lather, rinse, repeat." That's our entire life. It can seem so frustrating.

But think about the cycle. What do you get when you lather, rinse, and repeat?

Yes, you go through the motions, but you also get clean hair. The motions work. In fact, they are necessary. Without them, we can't grow. This is why we need to know the reason, the "why." Because at some point, if not already, the motions become monotonous. At some point, we will look at what we are doing and ask, What good is this? What use is this when it seems so meaningless and so mundane?

The motions work. In fact, they are necessary. Without them, we can't grow.

In the story of Naaman, which is recorded in 2 Kings chapter 5, Naaman, a general of the Syrian army, is more or less an enemy of Israel. He is wealthy, powerful, and successful, and he has a reputation for being a pretty good guy. But Naaman has a massive problem: he has leprosy. This basically means he has a death sentence hanging over his head. His wealth, power, success, and even his good reputation can do nothing to help him.

As the story unfolds, we learn that Naaman has a servant girl in his household whom he has kidnapped from her people, the Jews. This kidnap victim, who is now one of Naaman's slaves, says that there is a holy man in Israel, her homeland, who could heal him. Naaman doesn't think twice. He saddles up, gathers his entourage, and heads down to Israel (see 2 Kings 5).

When the king of Israel hears Naaman's request, he freaks out because he cannot heal leprosy. Elisha, the man of God, tells him not to worry and instructs him to send Naaman to his house.

As Naaman is journeying to Elisha's house, Elisha sends out his apprentice to tell Naaman to "go and wash in the Jordan seven times, and your flesh shall be restored, and you shall be clean" (2 Kings 5:10). Naaman is furious when he hears this message and does not want to follow these instructions. He doesn't understand why he had to go all the way there and not just bathe in the waters where he lived. He was expecting to be healed with the wave of a hand (see 2 Kings 5:11). But his servants encourage him to try it.

Before he gets in the water, Naaman says, "What is this going to do? What use is this?" This is where a lot of us are. If there is going to be a change, we expect it to be big. The apprentice even says to Naaman, "If the man of God asked you to do something extraordinary, like climb up the top of the mountain and dance around, you'd do it right away. But he just asked you to do something simple, something that seems meaningless, so why don't you do that?" (see 2 Kings 5:13).

We expect transformations to happen all at once in big, dramatic moments, or else we think that greatness is just inborn. So many of us accept this idea that greatness—genius—is something you're either born with or you'll never get. We don't expect to achieve it by just going through the motions.

THE MAKING OF A GENIUS

In the 1960s, a Hungarian educational psychologist named László Polgár decided to challenge the assumption that genius can only be born. He suspected that he could raise a genius, and to test this idea, he placed an ad in papers throughout Europe for a woman who was willing to marry him and have children. He wanted to experiment with their children to see if he could create geniuses. I am not saying this is ethical, but this is how it happened.

A woman from Ukraine answered his ad, and he married her. In 1969, they had their first daughter, Susan. László started looking for some area of challenge where his daughter could become a genius. It couldn't be something athletic (because he wasn't sure whether she would have physical prowess), and it couldn't be artistic (because he wanted it to be objective). He settled on chess. His theory was that any healthy child could become a genius with proper guidance, so he set out to train Susan in chess.

Greatness—genius—is not something you have to be born with.

When she was four or five years old, László took Susan to the local chess hall where some talented masters were playing. He asked if his daughter could play against them. She cleaned all of them out. In fact, Susan went on to become the first woman in history to win the World Chess Championship, to become a chess grandmaster, and to win the chess Triple Crown. She's incredible.

László's next daughter, Sofia, was born in 1974. She became one of the top one hundred chess players in the world. At one point, in the city of Rome, Sofia played against a bunch of chess grandmasters at once and single-handedly defeated all of them. They called this game The Sack of Rome, and it is ranked as one of the top five chess games in history.

But both Susan and Sofia were outstripped by their youngest sister, Judit. Every article I read about her said that you couldn't begin to describe all her victories, all her accomplishments, and all her achievements. She became a chess grandmaster at fifteen years and two months, making her the youngest person in history, at the time, to win this title. She was the first woman to beat the reigning world champion Garry Kasparov, who had previously said that there was no way a woman could ever beat him.

You can watch a video of this game online, and he is so upset that he gets up and walks away. It's pretty funny.

László was able to demonstrate that greatness, genius, is not something you have to be born with, nor is it the result of a massive movement or change. It is the result of going through the motions again and again. These girls said that their father never made them play chess. At first, they played because they just liked playing. But when they had the idea that they could do more than just play chess, when they realized they could be great at chess, that became the goal. Not to just play chess, but to be great at it, became their *why*.

MEANINGFUL, NOT MUNDANE

I wonder how many of us believe that greatness is possible. How many of us truly believe that God wants greatness out of us? How many of us really believe that God wants us to be saints? And not only that, but that it is *possible* for us to be saints?

We can say, "I get it. I can be a saint. Well, if I was born in the Middle Ages and didn't have a smartphone, I could totally be a saint." But are you convinced that God actually *wants* you to be a saint? Because he does. God wants you to become a saint simply by doing the same things that every other saint in history has done.

> God wants you to become a saint simply by doing the same things that every other saint in history has done.

When you go to Mass, you are doing the same thing that transformed the world of every saint God ever raised up. Does it feel like you are doing something saintly? Does it feel like you are doing something impressive? No, it feels so mundane. It feels so ordinary. It feels meaningless, like, I don't know, hopping in the Jordan River seven times. But when Naaman got in the Jordan River seven times, he was completely transformed.

When we hear the story of Naaman, we almost always connect it to the Sacrament of Baptism. Every year, people in RCIA go through the process of becoming Catholic and get baptized at the Easter Vigil. It's one of those situations that could appear underwhelming even though you realize it is a huge moment. When they get baptized, they stand by the baptismal font, lean over slightly, and the bishop pours a few trickles of water over their heads, saying, "I baptize you in the name of the Father, and of the Son, and of the Holy Spirit." And then they stand up, they dab their foreheads with a towel, and it's all over. It's a hugely impressive moment, but it looks like nothing happened. And yet, every time someone gets baptized, they are washed clean of original sin, made into a son or daughter of God, filled with the power of the Holy Spirit, and completely transformed. It's a massive change, but on the surface, it can look like a meaningless action.

Think about going to confession. Remember, although Naaman had strength, power, and success, he had one massive problem that he couldn't fix himself. When you go to confession, this is you, too. However blessed your life might be, however successful or powerful or fun or friendly you are, or however many people love you, if you find yourself falling into sin, you realize that there is a part of yourself that you can't fix on your own.

So what happens? You go into a little room on the side of the church. You say some words, and the priest waves his hand over you. Afterward, you might wonder, Am I done? Am I good? It doesn't feel like anything is happening, and yet in that moment, all your sins are wiped away. Not only that, but you are completely reconciled to the Father and to the Church. In that moment, you are given a special grace, a special strength to get up and move forward. But it can feel like you're just going through the motions.

Lastly, when you show up to Mass every Sunday, it can feel like you're simply going through the motions. But if you have a *why*—if you find a *reason* for all of this, I'm telling you—I'm promising you—that going to confession and Mass will never again feel like you're just going through the motions.

Here's a "why." I go to confession because I know it heals me, and so my "why" is that I want to be healed. Or maybe I go to Mass because I know that it gives me life, and so my "why" is I that want to be filled. Maybe I go to both confession and Mass because I want to be holy. All of these reasons are good. To want to be healed, to want to be filled, and to want to be holy are all really good "whys."

But why did Naaman go into the water? Sure, he wanted to be healed, but he went into the water because Elisha told him to.

I want to be healed, I want to be holy, and I want to be filled. These are all good "whys," but the deepest "why," the most powerful "why," is actually a "who." At the Last Supper, on his last night on earth before he died, Jesus took bread and said, "Take, eat; this is my body." He took a chalice filled with wine and said, "Drink of it, all of you; for this is my blood of the covenant" (see Matthew 26:26–28). Then he said to do this in memory of him. Why do we go to Mass? Because he asked us to. We can fall back into duty and obligation, and it might feel like a trap. Or maybe, it feels like love.

TURNING "WHY" INTO "WHO"

The movie *The Princess Bride* opens with a grandfather reading a story to his grandson, who is sick. The story begins with two main characters. The name of the female protagonist is Buttercup, and the male protagonist, who is a farm boy, is named Westley.

As the story begins, Buttercup keeps telling Westley what to do, and every time she gives him a command, Westley always responds with three words: "As you wish." If Buttercup said, "Farm boy, make me some tea," or "Put some logs on the fire," or "Fetch me that picture," Westley would say, "As you wish."[5]

The day came, though, when Buttercup realized that every time Westley said, "As you wish," he was really saying, "I love you." You see, every time he did what she was asking him to do, it wasn't obligation, it wasn't duty—he wasn't a slave, he was in love. Every time he did what she asked and said, "As you wish," it was an act of love.

The same is true for us. We go to Mass is because Jesus asked us to. Our "why" is a "who," even if you don't know him yet. Because there are so many people who are raised in the Church and have not yet met Jesus. So many of us who have not yet encountered the "who" who has won our hearts. If you don't know him yet, can your why still be a who? I think it can.

WHEN YOUR "WHY" IS LOVE

I recently spoke with a woman who said that when she was growing up, physical fitness wasn't very important to her. When she got to college, one of her Bible study leaders asked her, "God willing, if you have kids someday, do you want to be stuck on the sidelines watching them, or out there with them, being present, and moving with them?" She really thought about this. She realized that if she changed part of her lifestyle, she could be present with her kids someday.

And so she started being attentive to what she ate and how she moved. If you were to look at her, you might observe what she was doing and how she was doing it. But you would miss the point, because these details weren't what mattered, what mattered were the future children she was doing it for. Her "whys" were "whos" who had not yet even been born.

She had not yet met her "whos," and yet those "whos" in her future were powerful enough "whys" to change her life.

Come to Jesus in the sacraments—
because the goal is him, and the "why" is love.

We are asked to come to Jesus in the sacraments. He asks us to come to confession. He asks us to come to Mass. And we show up, and we do what we know how to do. We do it in a familiar way. But our "why" has to be a "who." I have to be there because Jesus wants me there. So we show up and we do these seemingly meaningless, mundane things, knowing that they actually are meaningful actions oriented toward a worthy goal, because the goal is him, and the "why" is love, and we know that we can grow through the motions when our "why" is a "who": Jesus.

REFLECT

Reflect on a time in your own life when knowing the "why" behind an action made a significant difference in how you approached the task.

Consider László Polgár's claim that genius does not need to be born but can be made. Do you think this is true? Are there any circumstances where you would disagree? Explain.

Reflect on the example of Westley in *The Princess Bride* saying "as you wish" as an act of love. How does this relate to our relationship with God and our willingness to participate in the sacraments?

Do you truly believe that God desires holiness for you? How do you personally view your potential for holiness?

PRAY

Though most of us would prefer to grow in our faith through unbelievable, exciting, and undeniable moments of closeness with God, he has instead chosen the small, mundane, and easily overlooked areas of our lives in which to draw us to him. He saves through water, forgives through confessing, and hides his very being behind bread and wine.

As you begin your time of prayer, realize that it's okay if prayer and the sacraments don't seem entertaining to you. It is normal to feel bored sometimes. It's understandable, because God has hidden his grandeur in the mundane, physical aspects of the sacraments and prayer. He seems veiled because he has veiled himself.

The challenge is that we must strive to do the simple things God has told us to do, simply for the love of him. Simply because he said so. Much like Naaman, we would prefer to climb a mountain, when all he is asking us to do is dunk in the water a few times. Your Father rarely asks you to walk on water, but he is daily asking you to talk to him, confess when you sin, and receive him into you. He is your "why." Because you love him, pray for the strength to do the easy things.

ACT ///

Make a point of attending daily Mass or going to confession this week.

CHAPTER 3

FULL RANGE OF MOTION

I have come to the conclusion that I have reached a new stage of aging. It's the stage where you make noises when you sit down and get up. When I get out of a chair or off the couch, I feel like I made it, like it's an accomplishment. Since this is a new moment in my life, I did some research on aging.

Many Americans who are sixty-five years old and older are limited in their ability to perform basic actions. Basic, everyday actions could include anything from picking something up off the floor to reaching for a box of cereal in the pantry. For the elderly, these movements are restricted.

As we get old, our muscle mass decreases, our bones become weaker, and our joints become more inflamed and in pain. And because of that, we begin to have what you call "limited mobility." The same thing happens when you get injured. You lose the ability to move in your full range of motion.

I read an article that described this. It said, "While we're young, we don't think about the fact that one day simply bending down to tie our shoes might become not only difficult, but dangerous." It went on to say that if we want to live independently when we are older, "every single daily functional movement required for independent living has to be maintained."[6] Some people go to the gym or exercise well into their sixties, seventies, and eighties. But to be able to do that, we need to have the functional movements that are necessary for daily living.

The article also said, "Without functional exercises designed to support a healthy range of motion and condition our bodies for daily life, we become susceptible to all sorts of injuries and detriments."[7] Another way to say this is, to function as we wish when we are older, we have to start functioning now. We must go through the motions to be *able* to go through the motions. Otherwise, we're not able to live with a full range of motion.

Have you ever heard of Ben Patrick? As a kid, Ben loved basketball and dreamed of playing for a Division 1 team. By the age of twelve, he had played so much basketball that his knees were already in pain. By the time he was fourteen or fifteen, he had multiple tears in his knees. When he graduated high school, he had even more tears in his knees and absolutely no college basketball prospects.

But he didn't want to stop playing basketball or being athletic. He found a methodology that encouraged him to train using movements that didn't cause pain, no matter how limited that range of motion might be. He would never push through the pain but would do as much as he could without it. So he started with a limited range of motion and increased it over time.

As Ben practiced this methodology, he increased his range of motion slowly and steadily. He went through these motions again and again. By the time he was twenty-three, not only could he dunk again, but he was recruited by a Division 1 college and offered a full-ride scholarship to play basketball for them. He actually didn't end up playing, but that's another story.

Ever since, though, he has coached thousands of people who thought they couldn't play their sport anymore because they had lost their range of motion. He was able to coach them back to a place where they had a full range of motion with the maximum amount of weight that they could possibly bear.

IN EVERY SEASON

This book is called *Growing Through the Motions*. In the last two chapters, we talked about how, in so many areas of life, relationships, and faith, we can feel like we're just going through the motions. If we're doing it right, we don't just *go* through the motions; we actually *grow* through the motions. These motions can help us move forward. In the last chapter, we talked about how we should not go through the motions just because we know how. Instead, we should do them for a reason, a "why," and our "why" is a "who." We go through the motions for Jesus, and this increases our love.

In this chapter, we will highlight the importance of not just going through the motions at certain times or in certain seasons. We need to be able to go through the motions in every season. Another way to say this is that we need to have a full range of motion.

It's one thing to be patient or generous when you feel like it. It's one thing to pray when you want to. It's another thing to be able to be patient and generous always. It's another thing to be able to pray, whether you feel like it or not. This can come as a rude awakening.

Think about how much easier it is to be kind, patient, and generous with strangers than with your family. Sometimes, spending time with your family serves as a reminder that you are not as patient or as generous as you thought. Because, out in the world, you get to be generous and patient when you want to be. At home, you often need to be generous and patient even when you don't want to be.

The ability to have a full range of motion means that I can be patient in season and out of season. It means that I can pray both when I feel like it and when I don't. I can show up and go through the motions, even when I am busy or stressed. If I can't do this, I have limited mobility.

These motions we go through in our faith, like the Mass, are eternal. The Mass will probably stay the same for the rest of your life. It changes very, very little. What *will* change is the season. What will change are the situations we find ourselves in. This is why St. Paul told Timothy, "Preach the word, be urgent in season and out of season" (2 Timothy 4:2). St. Paul is inviting Timothy to be able to go through the full range of motion.

PRAYING LIKE MOSES

In the Gospel of Luke, Jesus stresses the importance of being able to pray without growing weary (Luke 18:1–8). How do we do this? I think the answer is that we pray even when we're weary. How do we become capable of praying in every season? We pray in *this* season.

> How do we become capable of praying in
> every season? We pray in *this* season.

In the book of Exodus, there is a battle between the Israelites and the Amalekites (Exodus 17:8–16). When the Amalekites attack, Moses climbs a mountain and raises his hands to pray. Everyone Moses knows, everyone he loves is fighting—their lives are at stake—and as he was praying, he started to grow weary. He stayed on that mountain, praying over his people, praying for victory in the battle, despite his exhaustion.

He prayed until the Israelites won. How can we become capable, like Moses, of not running away when we become weary?

The reality is that one day, maybe sooner than you think, the people you love and the people who are counting on you will need you. They will need you to be able to stand in the breach for them. They will need you to be steadfast when everything else is falling apart. They will need you to be faithful when everyone else is running away.

How do we become steadfast? We can follow the advice St. Paul gave to Timothy. In 2 Timothy, St. Paul says, "But as for you, continue in what you have learned and have firmly believed, knowing from whom you learned it and how from childhood you have been acquainted with the Sacred Writings which are able to instruct you for salvation through faith in Christ Jesus" (2 Timothy 3:14–15). St. Paul knows Timothy; he knows that Timothy was raised in a Christian household.

PAUL'S CHARGE TO TIMOTHY

"I charge you in the presence of God and of Christ Jesus who is to judge the living and the dead, and by his appearing and his kingdom: preach the word, be urgent in season and out of season, convince, rebuke, and exhort, be unfailing in patience and in teaching. For the time is coming when people will not endure sound teaching, but having itching ears they will accumulate for themselves teachers to suit their own likings, and will turn away from listening to the truth and wander into myths. As for you, always be suffering, do the work of an evangelist, fulfil your ministry" (2 Timothy 4:1–5).

When Timothy was young, his mother and grandmother taught him Scripture. That's what St. Paul means when he says, "From childhood you have been acquainted with the Sacred Writings." His mother and grandmother taught him the Psalms, too, and he knew how to pray. He had also received the Eucharist.

St. Paul is telling Timothy to go through the motions he has been taught ever since he was a kid. Paul wants Timothy to be great, and so he tells him to pray the prayers his mother and grandmother taught him, to receive the Eucharist that they introduced him to, and to read the Scriptures that they told him about. Paul reminds him to go through these motions in season and out of season. The remarkable thing is that Timothy listened.

According to tradition, Timothy was martyred when he was eighty years old. He died as a man who had a full range of motion in his faith. He had this range of motion because he was preaching, and he did not stop preaching, even in the face of opposition. He knew what it meant to preach in season and out of season. He knew what it meant to pray in every season. He understood the importance of doing these things because he decided he was going to go through the motions, no matter what, in every season.

FALLING TO THE LEVEL OF OUR TRAINING

Not too long ago, the bishop gathered all the priests in our diocese for a formation week. During the week, the bishop visited with all the priests, including those who had retired. One of the retired priests, who might be the oldest in the diocese, was one of my priests when I was growing up in Brainerd, Minnesota, and he had seemed old even back then.

Now he is in assisted living and is mostly nonresponsive. The bishop said that he sat down with this priest, and as he was talking to him, he just wasn't responding. At one point, the bishop said, "Hey, Father, let's pray." In that moment, something switched, and all of a sudden, the retired priest was right there praying along with the bishop. When it was just conversation, he wasn't there, but the moment the bishop invited him to pray, the priest was fully present to him.

I don't know what was going on at that moment. It seems to me that in the midst of limited physical and cognitive mobility, this priest still had a full range of motion spiritually. When nothing else was left, he could still pray. It's incredible.

We get ready for *then* by acting *now.*

We could hear this story, or we could hear the story of Moses, and say, "Yeah, when it comes down to it, that's what I'll do. When people who love me are counting on me, I'll rise to the occasion. At the end of my life, I'll be able to pray at the drop of a hat." I don't know if that's true.

The ancient Greek philosopher Archilochus once said, "We do not rise to the level of our expectations, but we fall to the level of our training." The Navy SEALs often quote this line, and it's pretty famous. We don't rise to the challenge, but we fall to the level of our training, the level of our preparation. This means if I want to pray in all seasons, I need to start by praying in this season. It means if I want a full range of motion, I have to go through the motions now. It starts today. We get ready for *then* by acting *now.*

COMMITMENT

I think we can strive for three goals: commitment, consistency, and companionship.

The first is commitment. Why do we need commitment? If I look at this week ahead and say, "Well, I'm going to pray when I feel like it," then I am not praying in all seasons. I'm only praying in seasons where I feel like it.

But if, on Sunday night, I decide when I will pray and stick with it for that entire week, I would be showing commitment. This is necessary.

Years ago, in one of my first years as chaplain at the University of Minnesota Duluth, we had Holy Hour every morning. At Sunday Mass, one of the first weekends of the year, I invited the students to make an effort to show up for Holy Hour at least once a week. The next morning, these twin sisters—freshmen—showed up. They were on the track and cross-country team and were incredible runners and students, but at the time, I didn't know them at all.

For the first half of the Holy Hour, we sat there in silence. They didn't seem to know much about what was going on. The Eucharist was in the monstrance on the altar, but they didn't know what the monstrance was. Afterward, I said, "You guys, it's so great that you're here. What inspired you to show up this morning?" They said, "Because you told us to." I said, "Come back tomorrow," and they agreed.

I'm not going to say they had perfect attendance. But for the next four years, almost every single morning, you could count on those two sisters showing up and praying from 6:45 to 7:45 a.m. Their commitment to prayer didn't just change the four years of their college career, it charted the course for the rest of their lives. After college, they both ended up marrying. It charted the course for their marriages, for the children they are now raising, and for the professions they both went into. And all of this happened because they made a commitment: I'm going to show up.

Another student went to the FOCUS national conference a few years ago. He encountered the Lord in a new way there. When he came back, he told the leader of his Bible study that he wanted to make a Holy Hour once a week. The leader said, "That's good, but I think it would be better if you just did 20 minutes every day." The student agreed to try that instead. He started his freshman year, and now as a senior, he has become a leader on campus. He was completely transformed because he made the commitment and kept showing up. We can only have a full range of motion if we make the commitment ahead of time and actually show up.

My invitation is for all of us to find a time to show up and pray this week. Maybe at home, maybe in the car, but even better, in the presence of Jesus in Adoration. Find a church near you and make the decision to go pray in front of our Lord in the Eucharist. Making that commitment makes all the difference. You could also commit to going to one extra Mass each week. Just check the schedule at your church, but then make that commitment ahead of time so you can exercise your full range of motion and go not just when you feel like it but even when you don't.

CONSISTENCY

The second goal is consistency: showing up again and again. I think that we love intensity, going hardcore and all at once. But consistency beats intensity every time.

Consistency beats intensity every time.

A couple years ago, when I was saying Mass, I recognized an older gentleman in the front row. He used to teach where my little brother and sister went to medical school. I had heard stories about this guy, and here he was in church! How cool is that?

After Mass, he approached me and said, "Father, I'd like to talk to you."

He continued, "I was raised Catholic, and I haven't been to church for fifty years. But I'm here now. I think I need to reconnect with the Lord."

I replied, "That's a good idea."

He said, "I think I need to go to confession. Can I do that with you?"

"Yes, sir."

So he went to confession, and afterward, he asked, "What do I do now?"

And I replied, "Well, you know how to pray, right?"

He said, "Yeah, my parents taught me."

"Okay. Do that."

In that moment, he made a decision. He committed.

A year and a half later, he called and asked if we could meet again, so he could give me an update.

He said, "That confession changed my life. I've been back to church. Some of the things from my broken past that have plagued my life are gone now. But the most important thing is that every night, I pray for fifteen minutes."

I said, "What do you do?"

He said, "I just pray the prayers that my mom and dad taught me."

Remember what St. Paul said to Timothy? Do the things you were taught, do the things that you learned, do the things that you believe.

"Fifteen minutes a day," he said. "I would never have believed it, but I'm a new man. After one year of praying for fifteen minutes a day, I'm completely transformed."[8]

He was a ninety-three-year-old man, so it's not too late for you either. It's never too late, because consistency beats intensity every time. You show up again and again. When you fail, go back.

COMPANIONSHIP

The third goal is companionship, because when Moses grew weary as he prayed on top of that mountain, he wasn't alone. There were two people with him. So when you commit to going to Mass or adoration in the upcoming weeks, I challenge you to find one or two people who will do it with you.

A big part of this is accountability. It's nice to have someone you can check in with to make sure you both are fulfilling your commitment. But also, when you go with someone else, it's a lot more fun. Holy Hour and Mass are more enjoyable when you don't have to show up by yourself. Ask someone you love to go with you. Because we need each other. The people who love you need you.

We need to be working toward a full range of motion, with the maximum amount of weight that we can bear, because at some point, maybe sooner than you think, someone will need you to exercise your faith when they can't. Someone is going to need you to have that full range of motion, because they are struggling, because they are hurting. Very soon, someone might need you to remind them of God's patience and his goodness in their worst season. The only way we can be there in someone's worst season is if we learn how to show up in every season. We can only be there if we train ourselves to go through the motions, and *grow* through the motions, so that we can have full range of motion in every season.

REFLECT

Maintaining "functional movement" is as important for your faith as it is for your health. What are some practical ways you can exercise and strengthen your faith in your daily life?

The Greek philosopher Archilochus said, "We do not rise to the level of our expectations, but we fall to the level of our training." Reflect on the "training" you have received in your faith. In a time of crisis, what might "falling back on your training" look like for you?

Have you ever experienced the strength of someone else's support during a time of suffering? Discuss ways that you can support your friends and loved ones when the need arises.

This chapter connects the goals of spiritual commitment, consistency, and companionship to the stories of college students, a man at church, and Moses in the Old Testament. Think of three people in your own life who accomplish these goals and consider how you can apply their examples to your faith journey.

PRAY

In order to grow through the motions, you must make them a regular part of your life. We achieve this through commitment, consistency, and companionship. However, this is not always easy to do. Thankfully, you are not alone in this life. In fact, because the motions are what enable you to live in intimacy with God, he is eager to help and guide you.

As you begin your time of prayer, remember that though God wants you to have a full range of motion, he is also capable of working within the range of motion you currently have. Your ability to commit, be consistent, and find faithful companions might be limited. He understands and wants to work with you where you are. Spend time sitting with the Lord, letting him show you how you can move forward in these areas.

ACT ///

Find a church that offers daily Mass or Adoration at a time that works for you and commit to attending for three consecutive weeks. That's three separate occasions. If possible, find a "buddy" to go with you.

CHAPTER 4

BUSY OR PRODUCTIVE?

Have you ever noticed that if you ask someone how they're doing, the answer is the same almost every time? If you say, "How's it going?" the answer is almost always, "Good. I'm busy." That's everyone. If you look around our world, everybody seems to be busy. Here's the thing: everybody *is* busy, but not everybody is productive. It's not the same thing.

In the chapters of this book, we have highlighted the fact that so much of life is just showing up and doing the same thing all the time. You put in your time—get up, go to work, come home, go to bed, and do it all over again the next day—and you realize that so much of life is just going through the motions. Even when it comes to our faith, we can feel like we are simply going through the motions, but ultimately, if we realize that our actions are meaningful and oriented toward a worthy goal, then we are actually *growing* through the motions.

In chapter 2, we talked about how everyone needs a "why." Our "why" is a "who." The reason we are doing these things—the reason we go to Mass—is because Jesus himself asked us to go. Every time we say yes to this invitation, we are saying yes to him. And we are not only going through the motions, but we are also growing in our ability to love. Every time we attend Mass, we are exercising love.

Every time we attend Mass, we are exercising love.

In the last chapter, we talked about how we want to have a full range of motion when it comes to "the motions." That means going through the motions in every season. I become able to go through the motions in any season when I show up in every season. We can grow. We say yes to the Lord. He is our "why," and our "why" is a "who." We can attend Mass and practice our faith because we believe that repeated actions are amplified over time. Over time, they have a compounding effect.

Many of us hope to be great one day. Being great is actually pretty easy. It is simply being good over and over again. Ultimately, that's all it is, because repeated actions are amplified over time. So how do we become great? We go through the motions.

ROUTINES FOR FREEDOM

Daniel Kahneman, psychologist and winner of the Nobel Prize in Economics, has a book called *Thinking, Fast and Slow*. In it, he talks about two systems of thinking.

System 2 thinking is really deliberate. If we are thinking this way, we are being intentional. We are being logical. We are thinking through every step, which is taxing on our system. System 1 thinking is much easier. It's quick-thinking, which is reflexive. System 1 thinking is emotional, whereas System 2 is logical and deliberate.[9]

For example, if you drive a car, think back to when you started. First, you have to learn what the driver's seat feels like. You have to focus on holding the wheel at ten o'clock and two o'clock, remembering the difference between the windshield wiper and the blinker, using the mirrors, and getting a feel for the gas and the brake pedals. When you are on the road, you don't know what to pay attention to because you are deep in System 2 thought.

After about fifty hours of driving, almost everybody shifts into System 1. You get in the car, and you recognize the controls. You can tell the blinker apart from the windshield wiper. You know what to pay attention to and what to ignore. You go from the intense thought of System 2 to System 1, which is automatic. And then you have some freedom to just enjoy driving.

Doing an action over and over again takes us out of System 2 and brings us into System 1. So, going through the motions, having a routine, helps us have efficiency. You have probably heard about how Steve Jobs, the former CEO of Apple, would wear the same pair of jeans and turtleneck every single day. He was saying, essentially, "I don't have to make that decision every morning. I can use my mental energy to make other decisions."

In fact, I read somewhere about this minimalist who purged his closet a couple of years ago. He went from over three hundred articles of clothing to just thirty items. Now, he wears the same thing every day. He says he prefers it this way because (1) he has fewer decisions, (2) he spends less time and energy making those decisions in the morning, and (3) he has less stress because he starts his day off knowing exactly what he's going to do. He put a lot of thought up front into what his look would be, and he looks like that every single day. Now, he is free to think in System 1, where his repeated actions are amplified over time.

EFFICIENT OR EFFECTIVE?

Here's what this has to do with our faith. When it comes to prayer, we do the same thing every time. When you go to Mass, you know what's coming. One of the many reasons for this is because repeated actions are amplified over time. This means that we can focus past the actions—we don't have to think about the actions anymore but can see past them to the heart of what we are really doing.

I remember being told in seminary, "When you get ordained, you'll be saying Mass every single day, maybe a couple times a day." They said, "Just get ready. It will take over a year until you feel like you're actually able to pray the Mass." It's true. At first, almost every priest is wondering, "What do I do with my hands? What do I say? I don't know what I'm doing with all the ribbons in this book." But we keep saying Mass, and over time, it makes sense.

If you converted to the Catholic Faith, you probably know this feeling. You show up to Mass, and it looks like everyone knows the choreography, like everyone knows the moves. Maybe now, after you've been coming to Mass for a while, you finally don't have to think about what to do. You can enter into the Mass. You can pray. You have become efficient, and that's really, really good.

I have had coaches who would always tell us, "How you practice is how you play." So if you practice with bad form, you're going to play with bad form. If you cut corners when you practice, you're going to cut corners when you play, because repeated actions are amplified over time. We have to be careful how we practice. We also have to be real with ourselves: maybe I'm doing things right, but am I doing the right things? Even if I'm showing up, even if I'm efficient, am I doing the things that matter?

Peter Drucker, who is an author, teacher, and speaker, made the distinction between being busy and being productive. It's the same thing as being efficient or being effective. Famously, he said, "Effectiveness is the foundation of success. Efficiency is the minimum condition for survival after success has been achieved." He goes on to say, "Efficiency is doing things right. Effectiveness is doing the right things." Why? Because everyone is busy, but not everyone is productive. Everyone is capable of being efficient, but not all of us know what it means to be effective.

Many of us have had the experience of getting lost while driving and wondering, "Okay, am I on the right road?" We keep driving down the road, going faster and faster. But if I am on the wrong road, the faster I travel, the farther away I get from my destination. If I'm on the wrong road, no matter how efficient I am, I'm getting farther and farther off course with every passing moment.

> ## We are called to work hard. But there is nothing so worthless as working hard on the wrong things.

We all are busy. Am I busy *doing things right*, or am I productive, *doing the right things?* Take St. Paul. He was a busy man who worked hard his entire life. I think, in so many ways, he was a lot like us. His letter to Timothy contains our last record of his words. He was writing it at the end of his life.

In his letter, he said, "I am already on the point of being sacrificed; the time of my departure has come. I have fought the good fight, I have finished the race, I have kept the faith" (2 Timothy 3:6–7). St. Paul was efficient, but even better, he was effective. He didn't just run a race; he ran the right race. This is absolutely necessary. We are called to work hard. But there is nothing so worthless as working hard on the wrong things.

THE PROBLEM WITH SELF-RELIANCE

The Gospel of Luke has a picture of another hard worker. Jesus describes a Pharisee who is praying in the Temple area. If we know anything about Pharisees, we know that they were hard workers. The Pharisees were dedicated to the Law. In fact, they were committed to keeping all 613 laws in the Old Testament. Not only that, but they also wanted to keep all the oral laws that weren't written in the Old Testament. They were constantly vigilant. They were constantly busy.

This particular Pharisee goes into the Temple area and gives his credentials. He says, "I fast twice a week, I give tithes of all that I get" (Luke 18:12). If you're a Pharisee, you only have to fast once, and you don't have to pay tithes on your whole income, just on a portion of your income. This guy goes above and beyond. He is not just part of the busy crew; he is the busiest of the busy. The good news is that he is doing the work. He is going through the motions. But the motions do not help unless they are the right motions. What's more, going through the motions will grow us, but will it grow us in the way we want? Will we grow in the way God wants?

Author and speaker Stephen Covey described a phenomenon called "the ladder against the wall." He said that he works with so many successful people who have climbed the ladder of success, only to realize it was up the wrong wall. They got to the top and discovered that they didn't like the view. How we spend our time is how we spend our lives, so do not practice what you do not want to become.

What was the Pharisee's error? He worked hard, he was busy, but what did he do wrong? When Jesus described the scene, he said, "Two people went up into the temple to pray, one a Pharisee and the other a tax collector" (Luke 18:10). So far, so good. The Gospel goes on to say, "The Pharisee stood and prayed thus with himself, 'God, I thank you that I am not like other men'" (Luke 18:11). This indicates a bit about how he might have perceived himself. He showed up to the Temple area to pray to God, but he didn't pray to God, he prayed to himself. Then he describes his accomplishments: "I fast twice a week, I give tithes of all that I get" (Luke 18:12). Basically, the Pharisee is praying *to* himself, *about* himself. He is basically saying, "God, I thank you that I'm already a good person. I thank you, but I don't need you. I'm good." This is the heart of self-reliance.

Self-reliance can lead to self-righteousness. This is a sense of complete blindness to what God has already done in our lives and to the fact that we need God.

Paul's prayer is the exact opposite. At the end of his life, he could point to all the things he's accomplished. But as he's writing to Timothy, he says, "From now on there is laid up for me the crown of righteousness, which the Lord, the righteous judge, will award to me on that Day" (2 Timothy 3:8). Just a few verses earlier, he described how the Lord had delivered him and rescued him from evil throughout his life. As St. Paul is praying, he is writing about what God has done. It's not about himself. There's no trace of self-reliance. Essentially, he is saying, "All of this, all my life, every gift I have, is all because of God."

TO HIM BE THE GLORY

"But the Lord stood by me and gave me strength to proclaim the word fully, that all the Gentiles might hear it. So I was rescued from the lion's mouth. The Lord will rescue me from every evil and save me for his heavenly kingdom. To him be the glory for ever and ever. Amen" (2 Timothy 4:17–18).

So on the one hand, you have the Pharisee, whose self-reliance leads to self-righteousness. He's a good guy, a busy guy, but in the wrong way. On the other hand, you have the tax collector. He was not a good person, and he knew it. If he had tried self-reliance, he would have been led to self-condemnation.

IT'S NOT ABOUT ME

This is where a lot of us find ourselves. It's one or the other. When we look at our accomplishments, we can end up self-righteous, or if all we can see is our brokenness, we wonder: "Why am I not better? I'm working so hard. Why am I not holy already? I'm going through the motions. Why am I not a saint yet?"

The tax collector knew he was not a good guy, and so he knew he could not be self-reliant. Instead, he showed up and told the truth, saying, "God, be merciful to me a sinner!" (Luke 18:13). He knew that he couldn't be focused on himself. Whereas the Pharisee prayed to himself about himself, the tax collector prayed to God about his need for God, basically saying, "I have nothing to brag about." He avoids self-condemnation by leaning into humility. He leans into the reality that he knows himself, but he also knows God.

This is the critical thing: we can only avoid self-condemnation when we know our brokenness and know Jesus' mercy—when we know our failure, but also know his victory. Our temptation, too often, is to focus on ourselves, whether that be on our strengths or on our weaknesses. We think, "I need to fix myself; I need to untangle these knots on my own, I need to prove myself." Jesus invites us to stop trying to figure it all out. He says, "You're busy doing the wrong thing." Jesus invites us to look at our wounds and then look at him and invite him into the wounds. That is what changes our hearts.

> We can only avoid self-condemnation when we know our brokenness and know Jesus' mercy.

You might be wondering, How can I tell if I have a Pharisee's heart or a tax collector's heart? What can I do? Because I don't want to just be busy,

I want to be productive. I want to be effective. I don't just want to do things right; I want to do the right things.

Have you heard of the Litany of Humility? It's a prayer that some churches print in their bulletins, but you can also find it at the end of this chapter. The Litany of Humility is a list of requests to Jesus. It starts off by saying, "O Jesus! Meek and humble of heart, make my heart like yours." And after every line, you pray: "Deliver me, O Lord."

It goes on: "From the desire of being esteemed, deliver me, O Lord. From the desire of being loved, deliver me, O Lord. From the desire of being honored, deliver me, O Lord. From the desire of being preferred to others, deliver me, O Lord. From the desire of being consulted, deliver me, O Lord. From the fear of being humiliated, deliver me, O Lord. From the fear of being forgotten, deliver me, O Lord. From the fear of being wronged or abandoned, or being refused, deliver me, O Lord."

"That others may be loved more than me, Jesus, grant me the grace to desire it. That others may be esteemed more than me, Jesus, grant me the grace to desire it. That others may be praised, and I go unnoticed, Jesus, grant me the grace to desire it."

And lastly, "Lord, I want to rejoice at being unknown and poor. When people do not think of me, Lord, I want to rejoice. When they assign me to the meanest tasks, Lord, I want to rejoice. When they never ask my opinion, Lord, I want to rejoice."[10]

My invitation to you is to pray the Litany of Humility provided at the end of this chapter every day for one week. If anything matches the definition of going through the motions, it's praying a litany. If any litany can help you grow through the motions, it's the Litany of Humility. Pay attention to the words because it is difficult. Praying it will be tough because if you have any self-reliance, it will be revealed; if you have any self-righteousness, it will be exposed; and if you have any self-condemnation, it will be healed.

I'm leaving you with this challenge because I can think of no better, surer way to make sure we're not just doing things right, but actually doing the right things. That we're not just busy, but productive. That we're not just efficient, but effective. Pray the Litany of Humility once a day this week and remember that you are not just going through the motions, but with God's grace, you are actually growing through the motions.

REFLECT

Being busy and being productive are two separate things. How can you discern whether you are truly being productive in your daily activities, or whether you are simply distracting yourself with busyness?

Actions become amplified when they are repeated over time. Have you experienced the compounding effect of consistent spiritual practices in your life? Discuss.

This chapter emphasizes the distinction between doing things right and doing the right things. How do you discern what actions align with God's will and purpose for your life?

Explain the difference between System 1 thinking and System 2 thinking. What advantages could System 1 thinking give you in your spiritual routines?

PRAY

You probably find yourself spread too thin, frazzled in your mind, and too busy to slow down. Most people feel this way. As you begin your time of prayer, give the Holy Spirit time to speak to your heart about areas where you may be busy, but not productive. Ask God to show you the ladders you should climb down from. Openly and honestly give God time to show you where, though you are running the race well, you are running the wrong race, and be prepared to make the necessary changes.

Next, allow the Lord to show you where you're either self-reliant or self-condemning. Where are you avoiding your wounds, or where are you too focused on them? Either way, spend time with God dwelling on what he reveals. It is normal to make mistakes in your life, and God understands. Thankfully, he is the remedy for both errors. You are too wounded to rely on yourself; and he is too merciful for you to waste time focusing on those wounds.

ACT ///

Pray through the Litany of Humility provided here. As you pray it, take time to think about each thing you're asking God for. Then, throughout the week, pray it every day, and allow yourself to be honest with God about the parts of the litany that scare you or make you nervous.

LITANY OF HUMILITY

O Jesus, meek and humble of heart,

Make my heart like yours.

From self-will, deliver me, O Lord.

From the desire of being esteemed, deliver me, O Lord.

From the desire of being loved, deliver me, O Lord.

From the desire of being extolled, deliver me, O Lord.

From the desire of being honored, deliver me, O Lord.

From the desire of being praised, deliver me, O Lord.

From the desire of being preferred to others, deliver me, O Lord.

From the desire of being consulted, deliver me, O Lord.

From the desire of being approved, deliver me, O Lord.

From the desire to be understood, deliver me, O Lord.

From the desire to be visited, deliver me, O Lord.

From the fear of being humiliated, deliver me, O Lord.

From the fear of being despised, deliver me, O Lord.

From the fear of suffering rebukes, deliver me, O Lord.

From the fear of being calumniated, deliver me, O Lord.

From the fear of being forgotten, deliver me, O Lord.

From the fear of being ridiculed, deliver me, O Lord.

From the fear of being suspected, deliver me, O Lord.

From the fear of being wronged, deliver me, O Lord.

From the fear of being abandoned, deliver me, O Lord.

From the fear of being refused, deliver me, O Lord.

That others may be loved more than I, Lord, grant me the grace to desire it.

That, in the opinion of the world, others may increase and
I may decrease, Lord, grant me the grace to desire it.

That others may be chosen and I set aside, Lord,
grant me the grace to desire it.

That others may be praised and I go unnoticed, Lord,
grant me the grace to desire it.

That others may be preferred to me in everything, Lord,
grant me the grace to desire it.

That others may become holier than I, provided that I may
become as holy as I should, Lord, grant me the grace to desire it.

At being unknown and poor, Lord, I want to rejoice.

At being deprived of the natural perfections
of body and mind, Lord, I want to rejoice.

When people do not think of me, Lord, I want to rejoice.

When they assign to me the meanest tasks, Lord, I want to rejoice.

When they do not even deign to make use of me, Lord, I want to rejoice.

When they never ask my opinion, Lord, I want to rejoice.

When they leave me at the lowest place, Lord, I want to rejoice.

When they blame me in season and out of season, Lord,
I want to rejoice.

Blessed are those who suffer persecution for justice's sake,
for theirs is the kingdom of heaven.

Amen.[11]

REMEMBER

- Growing through the motions means doing our duty and putting our whole heart into it.

- We receive the sacraments because Jesus told us to. We do the seemingly mundane tasks of spiritual life for the love of him. Our "why" is a "who."

- Commitment, consistency, and companionship enable us to grow through the motions and have full range of motion in every season.

- God's mercy can help you be not just busy, but productive. Effective, not just efficient. Humility takes our eyes off our own wounds and efforts and places them on God and his infinite mercy.

NOTES

1   Theodore Dalrymple, "A Sense of Duty Unsurpassed," *City Journal*, September 9, 2022, city-journal.org.

2   *The Karate Kid*, directed by John G. Avildsen (Columbia Pictures, 1984).

3   Malcolm Gladwell, *Outliers: The Story of Success* (London: Penguin UK, 2008).

4   Simon Sinek, *Start with Why* (Harlow, England: Penguin, 2021).

5   *The Princess Bride*, directed by Rob Reiner (Act III Communications, 1987).

6   "How to Support a Healthy Range of Motion in Active Older Adults," *HUR USA*, September 19, 2019, hurusa.com.

7   "How to Support a Healthy Range of Motion."

8   This is the retelling of a dialogue between the author and someone he encountered in his ministry.

9   See Daniel Kahneman, *Thinking, Fast and Slow* (New York: Farrar, Straus & Giroux, 2013).

10 Attributed to Rafael Merry del Val (1865–1930), cardinal and secretary of state under Pope St. Pius X.

11 Attributed to Rafael Merry del Val.